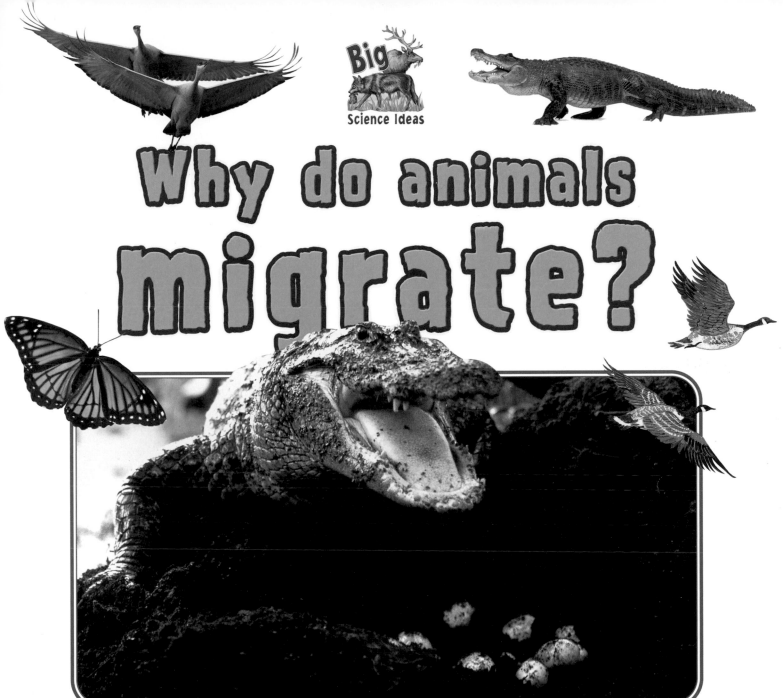

Big
Science Ideas

Why do animals
migrate?

Bobbie Kalman

🌳 Crabtree Publishing Company

www.crabtreebooks.com

Big Science Ideas

Created by Bobbie Kalman

For Magdalena and Otto,
our favorite migrating couple,
with love from Peter and Bobbie

Author and Editor-in-Chief
Bobbie Kalman

Research
John Crossingham

Editor
Kathy Middleton

Proofreader
Crystal Sikkens

Design
Bobbie Kalman
Katherine Berti
Samantha Crabtree (cover)

Production coordinator
Katherine Berti

Illustrations
Katherine Berti: pages 6, 18
Antoinette "Cookie" Bortolon: pages 14 (right), 15 (left), 31 (top)
Bonna Rouse: pages 1, 27, 31 (middle)
Margaret Amy Salter: pages 14 (left), 15 (right)

Photographs
© BigStockPhoto.com: pages 15 (bottom right), 23 (except inset)
© Dreamstime.com: page 1 (middle)
© iStockphoto.com: pages 20 (bottom), 23 (inset), 27 (bottom), 29 (top right)
© Shutterstock.com: front cover, pages 1 (except middle), 3, 4, 5, 6, 7, 8, 9, 10,
    11, 12 (right), 13, 14, 15 (except bottom right), 16, 17, 18, 19, 21, 22, 24, 25, 26,
    27 (except bottom), 28, 29 (except top right), 30, 31
© Wikimedia Commons: Bruce McAdam: page 12 (left)
Other images by Digital Vision

Library and Archives Canada Cataloguing in Publication

Kalman, Bobbie, 1947-
    Why do animals migrate? / Bobbie Kalman.

(Big science ideas)
Includes index.
ISBN 978-0-7787-3283-9 (bound).--ISBN 978-0-7787-3303-4 (pbk.)

    1. Animal migration--Juvenile literature. I. Title. II. Series: Kalman,
Bobbie, 1947- . Big science ideas.

QL754.K34 2009   j591.56'8   C2009-901256-1

Library of Congress Cataloging-in-Publication Data

Kalman, Bobbie.
  Why do animals migrate? / Bobbie Kalman.
    p. cm. -- (Big science ideas)
    Includes index.
    ISBN 978-0-7787-3303-4 (pbk. : alk. paper) -- ISBN 978-0-7787-3283-9
(reinforced library binding : alk. paper)
  1. Animal migration--Juvenile literature. I. Title. II. Series.

QL754.K35 2009
591.56'8--dc22

2009008009

Crabtree Publishing Company
www.crabtreebooks.com   1-800-387-7650

Copyright © **2009 CRABTREE PUBLISHING COMPANY**. All rights reserved. No part of this publication may be reproduced, stored in a retrieval system or be transmitted in any form or by any means, electronic, mechanical, photocopying, recording, or otherwise, without the prior written permission of Crabtree Publishing Company. In Canada: We acknowledge the financial support of the Government of Canada through the Book Publishing Industry Development Program (BPIDP) for our publishing activities.

Published in Canada
Crabtree Publishing
616 Welland Ave.
St. Catharines, Ontario
L2M 5V6

Published in the United States
Crabtree Publishing
PMB16A
350 Fifth Ave., Suite 3308
New York, NY 10118

Published in the United Kingdom
Crabtree Publishing
White Cross Mills
High Town, Lancaster
LA1 4XS

Published in Australia
Crabtree Publishing
386 Mt. Alexander Rd.
Ascot Vale (Melbourne)
VIC 3032

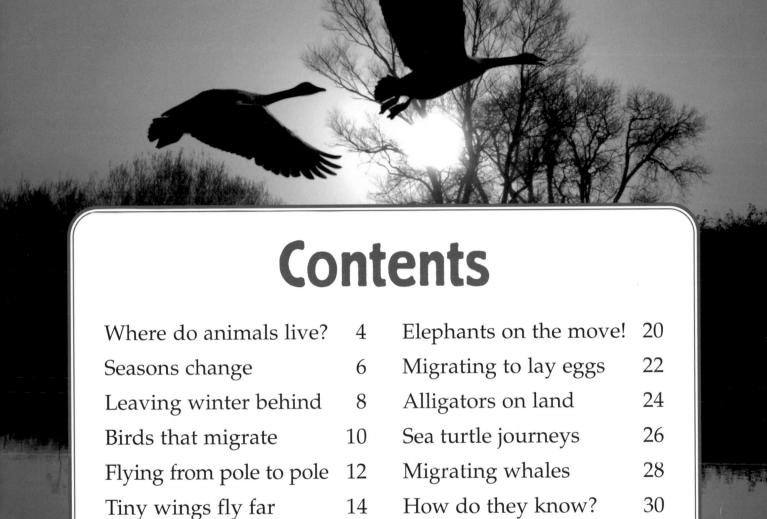

Contents

Where do animals live?

All animals have areas where they live. These areas are called **habitats**. In its habitat, an animal can find everything it needs to stay alive. It can find food, water, and shelter. Animal habitats are in forests, deserts, grasslands, and oceans. The sea turtle below lives in an ocean.

Climate

An animal must be able to survive in the habitat's **climate**. Climate is the usual weather in an area. Weather is made up of wind, temperature, and **precipitation**. Precipitation is water that falls from clouds as rain or snow.

This bear is getting soaked by rain.

Reindeer live in northern areas, where winters are very cold. Snow is part of the weather.

Seasons change

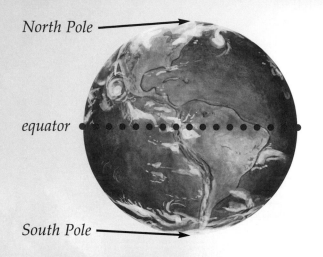

North Pole

equator

South Pole

Polar areas, which are near the North Pole and South Pole have long, cold winters and short, cool summers. Near the **equator**, the weather is always hot. The equator is an imaginary line around the middle of Earth. The hot areas near the equator are called **tropical** areas.

Wet and dry seasons

In many tropical areas, there are two main **seasons**. Seasons are periods of time with certain weather and temperatures. One season is the **wet season**. In the wet season, a lot of rain falls. The other season is the **dry season**. In the dry season, very little rain falls.

This sloth lives in a tropical rain forest. Rain is falling on its fur. In some rain forests, it rains almost every day.

Four seasons

Areas that lie between polar areas and tropical areas are called **temperate** areas. Temperate areas have four seasons—spring, summer, autumn, and winter.

What is migration?

When seasons change, it becomes difficult for some animals to stay in their habitats. These animals **migrate**. To migrate means to move to a new habitat for a certain amount of time.

*Canada geese are birds that migrate when the seasons change. These birds migrate in groups called **flocks**. In summer, Canada geese live in Canada and in the northern parts of the United States. In autumn, the geese fly to the southern United States and northern Mexico. These places have much warmer winters than Canada has.*

Most migrating animals make a two-way trip each year from one place to another and back again.

7

Leaving winter behind

In winter, many animals may not be able to survive the cold weather, or their food may be buried under snow. These problems force some animals to migrate to warmer habitats. The animals often migrate in autumn. When the weather gets colder, they know it is time to leave. The animals shown on these pages migrate to leave winter behind.

To where do monarch butterflies migrate in winter? (See page 14.)

Arctic terns

What helps sandhill cranes find their way? (See page 11.)

ruby-throated hummingbird

Which bird flies the farthest? Is it the hummingbird or the Arctic tern? (See pages 11-13.)

Warmer habitats

Animals that leave winter behind fly or walk to habitats that are warmer. Warmer areas also have more food and water. When the weather becomes warm in spring, the animals return to the habitats they left behind. Elks live high on mountains in summer and in **valleys** in winter. Valleys are low areas of land between mountains or hills.

Birds that migrate

Many of the animals that migrate to warmer places are birds. Birds do not all migrate the same way, however. Canada geese migrate in V-formation. Flying in V-formation keeps the geese from getting too tired. As the geese flap their wings, ripples are sent through the air behind them. The ripples are called **upwash**. Birds flying at the back of the "V" are lifted by the upwash of air, so they do not have to flap their wings as hard.

As they migrate, Canada geese constantly switch positions from the back of the "V" to the front. By switching positions, every goose gets to rest its wings in the upwash of air.

Sandhill cranes

Sandhill cranes live in Alaska, Canada, and in the northern and western parts of the United States. In winter, they migrate to the southern United States and northern Mexico. Birds with large wings, such as cranes, fly over land as much as possible, so they can **soar**, using air currents called **thermals**. To soar is to fly high without flapping the wings. Thermals are warm upward currents of air that carry birds high into the sky.

Ruby-throated hummingbird

Ruby-throated hummingbirds are tiny birds that travel great distances. Most migrating hummingbirds must stop often to feed at flowers or at feeders, even during migration, but ruby-throated hummingbirds cannot stop. They fly over the Gulf of Mexico, which is a huge area of ocean. There is no place to land, so the hummingbirds have to keep flying. Before they start migration, the hummingbirds fatten up by eating insects and drinking a lot of nectar. They nearly double their body weight before they start their journeys.

Flying from pole to pole

The Arctic tern migrates farther than any other animal! Terns are almost always traveling. In June, they live in areas near the North Pole. They lay their eggs and raise their young there. By August, terns begin their long journeys south. By December, they reach the areas near the South Pole, at the other end of Earth! The terns then begin flying north again after a few months of rest.

Arctic terns lay eggs on the ground. The eggs have colors and patterns that blend in with the stones and plants of the Arctic land.

A fluffy tern chick has hatched from one of the eggs. Chicks grow quickly so they can migrate with their parents in a few months. In the next 12 months, the chick will fly 25,000 miles (over 40,000 km).

12

Year-round sunshine

Summer happens at different times in different parts of Earth. In the northern part of the world, summer lasts from June to August. Arctic terns live in these polar areas during this time. In the southern part of Earth, summer is from December to February. The Arctic tern reaches the southern polar areas at this time. The Arctic tern has two summers every year!

Arctic terns eat mainly fish, which they catch by diving into oceans. They migrate along **coastlines** *so they can find enough food to eat. Coastlines are where oceans meet land.*

13

Tiny wings fly far

Monarch butterflies migrate when the weather gets cool in autumn. They travel from Canada and the northern United States to the southern United States and Mexico. When they reach their winter homes, thousands of monarchs land on trees and cover their branches. The butterflies then **hibernate** on the trees. To hibernate is to go into a deep sleep.

monarchs hibernating

Finishing the journey

In spring, the monarchs wake up from hibernation. They then fly north to their summer habitats. Some butterflies stop to **mate** along the way. They lay their eggs and soon die. A caterpillar **hatches** from each egg. It grows into a pupa and then into a butterfly. The new butterfly continues the migration north, back to where its mother started her journey.

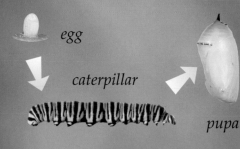

egg

caterpillar

pupa

chrysalis

green darner
dragonfly

A few types of dragonflies also migrate. Some green darner dragonflies leave the northern parts of North America and fly to the southern United States and back again.

Migration in the north

In summer, caribou live on the **tundra** and eat the plants that grow there. Before winter begins, hundreds of thousands of caribou migrate to the forests that are south of the tundra. In the forests, the trees block much of the snow from falling to the ground. The caribou use their hooves to dig under the snow to find food.

cone

The tundra is flat, treeless land near the North Pole. It has short summers and long, freezing winters.

16

Following food

Wolves live on the tundra and hunt caribou. When the caribou migrate, the wolves follow them. They hunt the caribou along the migration route. In summer, the caribou return to the tundra. The wolves that followed them return to the tundra, too.

Looking for fresh grasses

Wildebeest are animals that live on **savannas** in Africa. Savannas are huge areas of land, where many types of grasses grow. **Herds**, or big groups, of wildebeest feed on the grasses. Savannas are in the tropical areas of Earth, so they have wet and dry seasons. When the wildebeest have eaten all the grasses in one area, they move to another area where it has rained, and new grasses are growing. More than a million wildebeest cross the Mara River each year to find fresh grasses on the other side.

Animals such as zebras often migrate with the wildebeest. Zebras also eat grasses and other plants. All the animals shown above will cross the Mara River to find new grasses to eat.

*Each year, almost a half-million wildebeest calves are born between late January and mid-March. This newborn calf is **nursing**, or drinking its mother's milk.*

*Wildebeest and zebras are never safe from **predators**, such as lions. Predators hunt and eat other animals.*

Elephants on the move!

Elephants migrate to find food and water. They eat huge amounts of grass, bushes, and other plants to keep their big bodies alive. Elephant herds must now travel long distances to find enough food to eat because their habitats have been taken over by people. Farms have been built on the lands where elephants once found food.

(above) Asian elephants often come into villages and farms and eat the **crops** that people grow for food. Some farmers kill the elephants that eat their crops.

(left) These African elephants have wandered into a farm area looking for food. An electric fence has been put up to keep elephants out. The baby has gone under the fence, but the mother cannot get through. The baby may die without its mother's care.

21

Migrating to lay eggs

This toad lives in a forest. It is a long way from the pond where she will lay eggs.

eggs

The toad has laid eggs in the pond where she hatched. The eggs are all around her.

Frogs, toads, and salamanders are animals called **amphibians**. Amphibians start their lives in water and live on land after they become adults. Amphibians hatch from eggs. After the babies hatch, they grow into tadpoles, and then into adults that can also make babies. When it is time for the adults to lay eggs, they migrate back to the places where they hatched. They lay eggs and then return to the habitats in which they usually live. Frogs and toads migrate across land to the ponds where they hatched. Salamanders live under the ground. They also migrate to lay their eggs. They lay their eggs in small pools.

eggs

tadpole

This frog has laid many eggs in a pond. Each black dot inside an egg will grow into a tadpole. Tadpoles grow into frogs. Growing from an egg to an udull is called a **life cycle**.

Spotted salamanders live mainly under ground. In spring, they climb above ground and migrate to pools of water that form when it rains. They lay their eggs in the pools. After laying their eggs, they return to their underground homes. **Larvae**, or babies, hatch from the eggs and grow in the pools over summer. By the end of summer, the pools dry up. The young salamanders then find their own homes under ground.

Alligators on land

Some **reptiles** migrate to lay eggs, too. Alligators are reptiles that live most of their adult lives in water. They live in rivers, swamps, and lakes. Female alligators do not lay their eggs in water. They leave their water habitats to lay eggs on land. A female alligator builds a nest of grass and mud and lays her eggs inside. She covers the nest with plants and guards it until the eggs hatch.

egg tooth

*Each baby alligator breaks its egg using an **egg tooth**. The egg tooth is a hard bump on its snout. Before hatching, the babies let out loud noises to let their mother know that they are ready to hatch. The mother then digs out the eggs.*

Alligator mothers carry their babies back to the water and look after them for up to two years.
This alligator mother is carrying her babies on her back.

*Young alligators form **pods**, or groups.*

Sea turtle journeys

Sea turtles live in oceans, but they lay their eggs on land, just as alligators do. The turtles mate in the ocean. When the female turtle is ready to lay eggs, she makes a very long journey. She migrates to the same beach where she hatched from an egg. This beach is called the turtle's **natal** beach. There are seven **species**, or kinds, of sea turtles. The leatherback sea turtle is the largest and travels the farthest.

Some sea turtles migrate over 1,500 miles (2,415 km) to lay their eggs. This mother leatherback is crawling up the beach to find a spot to lay her eggs. She will then dig a hole.

1

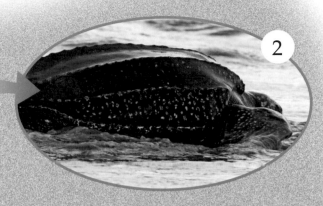

2

The turtle lays up to 150 eggs in the hole she dug. She covers the eggs with sand.

The mother leatherback leaves the eggs and swims back to her home. She will never see her babies.

3

When the eggs hatch, the **hatchlings**, or babies, start digging themselves out of the hole.

5

4

As adults, these turtles will swim back to this beach to lay their eggs.

Almost all the eggs have hatched. The hatchlings will now crawl to the ocean.

27

Humpback whales spend their summers in cold ocean waters near the North Pole. Cold ocean waters are full of tiny animals called **krill**. Whales eat krill, which keeps a lot of fat on the bodies of the whales. This fat is called **blubber**. Blubber keeps the whales warm in the cold waters. Whales migrate to warm oceans in winter to have babies. Adult whales live off their blubber.

baleen

*Humpbacks are called **baleen** whales because they have baleen instead of teeth. Baleen are long strips of bone that are used to trap krill from sea water. Before they migrate, humpback whales eat a lot of krill and put on blubber. They will not eat again for many months!*

Humpback whales migrate in autumn to mate and have **calves**, or babies. Calves have thin blubber when they are born, so mother whales must swim to warm ocean waters to have their babies. The calves would freeze to death if they were born in the cold waters near the North Pole.

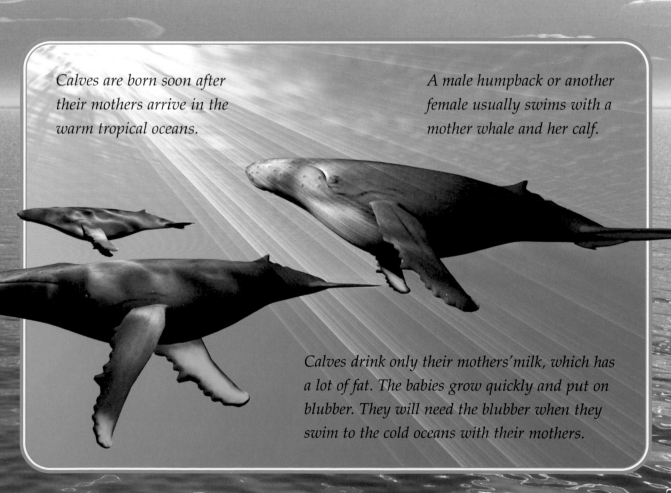

Calves are born soon after their mothers arrive in the warm tropical oceans.

A male humpback or another female usually swims with a mother whale and her calf.

Calves drink only their mothers' milk, which has a lot of fat. The babies grow quickly and put on blubber. They will need the blubber when they swim to the cold oceans with their mothers.

29

How do they know?

Most animals that migrate are not taught where to travel by their parents. Instead, they know by **instinct**. Instinct means that the animals are born knowing how, when, and to where they should migrate. Animals seem to use several ways to find their way as they move from one place to another.

compass

*Birds, such as this migrating white stork, may have built-in compasses that tell them in which direction they are flying. Birds that fly over land may also recognize **landmarks**. Landmarks are the different shapes of the land that birds see below them while they are flying.*

30

Using information

Animals use information from the Earth, sky, and oceans to **navigate**, or locate where they are and in which direction they are traveling. Most animals use more than one type of information. They may follow coastlines or see the position of the moon or stars. They might smell different odors in the oceans or follow water **currents**.

Monarch butterflies use the position of the sun in the sky to fly in the right direction.

Sea turtles use the sun and stars as guides. They also use their sense of smell.

Some animals, such as elephants, have fewer instincts than others. The young animals learn where to migrate by following the older animals in their herds.

Glossary

Note: Some boldfaced words are defined where they appear in the book.

amphibian An animal that lives the first part of its life in water and its adult life on land

climate The usual weather that an area has had for a long time

coastline The outline of areas where oceans meet land

crops Plants people grow for food

current Water moving in a certain direction

habitat The natural home of an animal

hatch To break out of an egg

hatchling A baby animal that just hatched

life cycle The set of changes a living thing goes through until it becomes an adult that can make other living things

mate To join together to make babies

natal Relating to a place or time of birth

navigate To follow a route of travel

polar Relating to areas that are near the North or South poles

predator An animal that hunts and eats other animals

reptile An animal with scaly skin, such as a snake, lizard, alligator or crocodile, or turtle

savanna A hot grassy land with a few trees

species Types of animals that can make babies together with their own kind

temperate Describing areas that are between the poles and equator

upwash Air ripples created by the wings of birds that make it easier for other birds to fly behind them

valley Low land between mountains or hills

Index

Printed in the U.S.A.—BG